This book belongs to...

_____

GROLIER
B O O K S
BOOK CLUB EDITION

For Walker Boyd

Did you know that your father,
Before you were around,
Used to ride on the subway
Upside down?

Library of Congress Cataloging-in-Publication Data:
Schade, Susan.
Toad eats out / by Susan Schade and Jon Buller.
   p.   cm. — (Step into reading. A Step 1 book)
SUMMARY: Toad's friends have a surprise birthday party for him at his favorite restaurant.
ISBN 0-679-85009-0 (trade) — ISBN 0-679-95009-5 (lib. bdg.)
[1. Restaurants—Fiction. 2. Birthdays—Fiction. 3. Animals—Fiction.
4. Stories in rhyme.] I. Buller, Jon ill. II. Title. III. Series: Step into reading. Step 1 book.
PZ8.3.S287Tm 1995 [E]—dc20 94-5285

Manufactured in the United States of America 10 9 8 7 6 5 4 3 2 1

TOAD EATS OUT

By Susan Schade and Jon Buller

BEGINNER BOOKS

A Division of Random House, Inc.

It's my birthday!
I can do what I want.

I want to eat
in a restaurant!

I pick up Bug.

We drive around.

The rides are fun
at FOOD PLAYGROUND.

They have good fries
at HOT DOG POWER.

We like the clown
at PANCAKE TOWER.

Where do we go?
Where we always do!
Our favorite place,
the CHEW AND VIEW!

We're hungry now!

What luck! A spot!

Here we come,
ready or not!

A table for Toad,
right this way.
Bee will be
your server today.

Hey! Cat is here,
and all the guys.
I am amazed!
They shout...

We all put on
our birthday caps.

We spread our napkins
in our laps.

The menu here
is very big.

What are you
having, Pig?

MENU

MEATBALL SOUP
JUMBO GUMBO À LA PAT
CLAM HASH
SLUMGULLION STEW
HUSH PUPPIES AND EGGS
PUMPKIN FRITTERS

What's Jumbo Gumbo
à la Pat?

I don't know.
I'll try that!

Bee writes it down
in a little book.

He goes away
to tell the cook.

Rolls and butter,
water with ice,

plenty of forks—
this place is nice!

Here it comes!

Our food is ready.

Jumbo Gumbo

and spaghetti!

Hot buttered corn
and black-eyed peas.
Would you like
some grated cheese?
Yes, thank you.
And pepper, please.

I take a bite.

Mmm…yum, yum, yummy!

I eat and eat.

I fill my tummy.

A cake for me!

And candles, too.

And now...let's see
what's in that box.
A big balloon
and matching socks!
A book! A glove!
A model ship!

We're done. We pay.

We leave a tip.

We love to eat out.

We never say no.

Anytime, anyplace,

we're ready to go!